Dymchurch and Burmarsh
in old picture postcards

Paul Harris

European Library ZALTBOMMEL/THE NETHERLANDS

GB ISBN 90 288 6652 3

© 2001 European Library – Zaltbommel/The Netherlands

No part of this book may be reproduced in any form, by print, photoprint,
microfilm or any other means, without written permission from the publisher.

European Library
post office box 49
NL – 5300 AA Zaltbommel/The Netherlands
telephone: 0031 418 513144
fax: 0031 418 515515
e-mail:publisher@eurobib.nl

Introduction

Following the success of 'Dymchurch in old picture post-cards', first published in 1998, I have been asked by European Library to produce a second volume of such pictures. This has not been a difficult task, since as well as there still being a lot of potential material not included in the first book, more has subsequently come to light.

Once again the book explores old Dymchurch by moving from west to east, starting at High Knocke early last century and moving through the village to the small hamlet of Burmarsh, here pictorially presented in detail for the first time.

Other subjects pictured in the new book include the old casino at High Knocke, camping locally, various shops not included first time around and more about local fishing and kettlenets. Also covered are smugglers, floods, firework day parties, the picture house (yes, Dymchurch had its own cinema once!) the Deck Café and Checksfields garage. Here we additionally look at the various 1930s buildings in the locality and the ancient and much renovated Neptune Inn. Again, sports teams are featured, and the Burmarsh bellringers. Apologies in advance for any names I have missed out or got plain wrong.

The last part of the book contains a full photographic record of Burmarsh, possibly the longest established settlement on the Marsh dating back to early Saxon times.

As with any book of this kind strange paradoxes between past and present become obvious. In these pages we see a Dymchurch smaller quieter and slower paced than today. There were less amusements for holidaymakers, fewer residential houses and flats and only very light through traffic. Yet the village in days gone by had two banks, a wider variety of shops and a cinema!

I have had considerable help in preparing this volume and must thank those who gave their time, pictures and information to the project. I am particularly indebted to John (Jumbo) Wraight for assembling from his own and others collections the pictures I have used. Jumbo also provided invaluable information for the captions on sports teams in particular and other aspects of local history. In addition he liaised with other local collectors and historians.

I would like to thank local historian John Stacey for so generously supplying photographs and information for the Burmarsh section of the book.

Finally I hope this book fills any noticeable gaps left by the first volume and records something more of the area in bygone days for posterity and for the enjoyment of residents and visitors alike both new and long established.

Paul Harris, St. Mary's Bay 2001

1   A fine aerial view of the High Knocke area during the 1920s. The small building near the bridge across the dyke was the local abattoir. Beyond this both on the High Knocke site itself and along Mill Road can be seen extensive camping. Visitors to Dymchurch in those days usually camped, before the advent of modern caravan and chalet developments. To the right of the picture can be seen Martello Tower No. 25 with some military huts next to it. Where the car park now is next to the tower seems to be just undeveloped grassland.

2 This 1930s view entitled Dymchurch Club shows what was at one time the Silver Waves casino. The distinctive style of the building shows its 1930s origins. Built in 1934 this establishment has variously enjoyed life as the Martello Beach Hotel, the Seabourne Club and the aforementioned casino. Increasing housing development took place in the area from 1936 and continues to this day. The club building was demolished in 1963.

3 Here is a close-up of the extensive camping area seen distantly in picture number one. This is strung along the dyke bank at the bottom end of the road that runs from Dymchurch to St. Mary in the Marsh. This may well be a 1930s view and was taken from approximately where the Rosie Lee's fish n' chip restaurant now is. The dyke bank here is now fairly inaccessible.

CAMPING AT DYMCHURCH. 918.

4 This first W.E. Cooper shop in Dymchurch was situated at roughly the viewpoint of the previous photograph and first opened its doors in 1924. The building shown was built largely of asbestos, which of course today would be unthinkable!

5 This imposing building was both a guest house and restaurant at the time this picture was taken, and was known as the Martello, offering board, residence, luncheons and teas. It was pulled down in 1957 and the site at the time of writing is the Martello Fish and Chip shop. The small building advertising fish in the background was Henleys fish and chip shop and fishmongers then and is the Rosie Lee's café today. Some things don't change that much!

6   B.J. Francis groceries and provisions store and post office as it was in the 1920s. Previously the shop was Pope and Son Grocers and Drapers and is now two establishments, a greengrocers and the Wellworths toy, fancy goods and classic trophies shop. Some years ago renovations to the shop revealed a long hidden cellar below in which human remains were found. These have been linked to occasional reports of ghostly visitors in the shop!

7   Here we see the same store as Pope's with various people seemingly lined up for the photo-graph. Very intriguing is the little house, obviously very old, situated next to Pope's. It was seemingly a private house and is surrounded by a white picket fence in front of which is a collection of children. This building has long since vanished. The site is now occupied by a car park.

8   A High Street view shown on a postcard postmarked 1943. On the right we can see the grocers, also a post office with public telephone. The little house in the gap has gone by now. Beyond this can be seen Hambrook and Uden butchers. On the opposite side of the road the newsagent and tobacconists advertises an old favourite, Gold Flake. The centre of the road in this view is occupied by the new traffic island.

9 A 1930s photograph of Hambrook and Uden Family Butchers. Standing in the doorway is Percy Hambrook. In the next doorway is Grace Hambrook speaking to a friend. The shop closed in October 1992 and the premises are now a fishing tackle shop.

10 The circus comes to town! Here we see one of a troop of elephants being driven along Dymchurch High Street past Smiths stores. In days gone by when the circus moved on from place to place the elephants were herded on by foot. In the case of Dymchurch the circus would normally pass from here to either Hythe or New Romney. The elephants were then driven along the seawall, usually at 5 a.m. to the next venue. This appearance in the High Street was probably to publicize the presence of the circus.

11 This view of Mill Road appears on a card post-marked 1935. Of particular interest here are two buildings right at the end of the road. On the left is the old school house and beyond this the house with a window just under the roof, used by smugglers in days gone by as a lookout for the arrival of customs officers. On the right, opposite this house is Brewers Bros Carpentry Workshops, and the next building towards us was the Cat and Kettle, now Dr. Syns restaurant.

12 The building shown here near the bridge contained a herring hang. A herring hang was a place where the fish were washed and then laid out and mixed with salt. After twenty-four hours the herrings were washed again, this time the scales came off due to the action of the salt. When the fish were finally ready they were hung over the fire to be smoked ready for onward sale.

13 The substantial houses now known as Lilac Cottage, Malvern Villas and The Laurels in St. Mary's Road seen in earlier years. This hasn't changed that much today, though it is noticeable that the grass verges were not maintained then it seems. Also the road is not full of parked cars as today.

St. Mary's Road. Dymchurch.

14 In this view of Dunkirk End we see the ivy-covered house where smugglers used to hide in the chimney again using the little window at the top of the house to look out for the approach of customs officers. The white building on the right known as Stanley House in times past was occupied by an interesting resident, who had an unusual taste in pets. Apparently he had a pet turtle which he swam attached to a string in the nearby dyke.

Dunkirk End, Dymchurch

15   Flooding near Orgarswick Avenue during the early 1920s due apparently to a problem with the sluice gates, which became wedged open allowing the sea to flood into the dyke overflowing it onto nearby land. Bearing in mind the low-lying nature of Dymchurch it has been remarkably lucky not to have been flooded more often, though in February 2001 some properties were flooded by an overflowing dyke following record winter rainfall. The long white asbestos building is the Marshlands Hotel, which stood opposite Stanley House.

16 This picture shows Cyril Stevens, a station-master at Dymchurch in the 1950s at the Eastbridge crossing. He worked on the Romney Hythe and Dymchurch Railway for a number of years on the station in the summer, and on the track in the winter months. He and his family lived for several years in the station house adjoining the Dymchurch railway station.

17 A 1940s view of the Deck Restaurant next to the coastguard cottages. A typical example of between-the-wars-architecture the restaurant was built for a Mr. Church in 1936. Today the building houses an amusement arcade and a fish and chip shop.

18 Another early view of the Deck Restaurant referred to here as the Deck Café and named on its front as just The Deck. Note the seating on the roof. Across the road from the café can be seen a bomb-site, which dates this view to after the Second World War. The building to the left of the café was Sigrist and Collins garage, who also had their own coaches. In front, next to the bomb-site, can be seen their breakdown vehicle.

19 A beach scene, probably 1920s judging by the ladies fashions. Note the little changing huts and tents. Also we can see what appears to be three Martello Towers. Nearest is number 24, then used as a coastguard lookout and now open to the public in summer and run by English Heritage. Beyond this is number 25, which now stands in a car park. These were twin towers built to protect the sluice from enemy interference. This was once a Royal Observer corps post and it was here that the first V1 was spotted crossing the channel in 1944.

20 Here by their kettle-nets next to the sluice at Martello Tower number 25 are Joe Henley (nearest the net) and a friend. The picture was taken around 1935. Kettlenetting was practised particularly between the 1890s and the late 1950s. This form of trapnet fishing was particularly popular around the Romney Marsh and Sussex area. About the time this picture was taken there were four kettlenets in Dymchurch. The Henleys had two nets, one at the sluice as mentioned and one at Willop Basin. Fred Smith and Reg Woodland also had nets on Dymchurch beach. Two more kettlenets were in use at St. Mary's Bay owned by a Mr. Body and Ninety Flisher.

21 Boats on a Dymchurch beach somewhat different from today. Today the seawall has been more developed and heightened and the beach much denuded. Climate change is bringing us more severe storms and the wall is often damaged or overwhelmed by the sea, as in October 1999. During summer though the scene is still happy and carefree. However, boats are no longer beached here.

The Sands — Dymchurch   1260

22　A nice view of Dymchurch High Street in the early 1960s. Notice the two banks on the left, Barclays and Lloyds. Today there are none. Also on the corner on the right can be seen Wraights Stores where today there is a café. Just above the banks and estate agents you can see the Coronation Clock installed in 1936. In 2000 another clock was put up on the opposite side of the road to mark the millennium.

23 Years ago in Dymchurch Guy Fawkes Day on 5th November was marked by parades and festivities that went on all day and culminated in a firework display on land next to Martello Tower No. 25. This was one such parade during the 1950s. See the guy being pushed along by some boys. Also the early Automobile Association Motorcycle and sidecar.

24 A 1960s Guy Fawkes pageant behind the Ocean Inn. The theme was obviously the Wild West that year. One boy has a very effective outfit representing Leslie Charteris' Saint character, popular on television at the time. Just behind the farthest left of the seated girls the tall cowboy-hatted man is Don Chaffey, the producer of the Danger Man and The Prisoner television programmes. To the right is Vincent Ball, an actor who featured in the TV soap Crossroads and the film A Town Called Alice.

25 This bungalow on the corner of Orgarswick Avenue and Orgarswick Way was known as Sunny Corner and was built for the Checksfield family in 1936. The road here was at that time a cinder track and was not properly tar-macked until the early 1960s.

26 Hardens shop, a local grocers, greengrocers and general stores, between 1949 and 1958 run by Cyril and Norah Harden. They had an additional outlet on the Pipers Camping and Caravan site and operated the only van delivery service in the area.

TRY OUR
SERVICE

HARDENS
OF DYMCHURCH.

AND BE
SATISFIED.

phone 336

27 The W.E. Cooper outfitters and drapers on the corner of Orgarswick Avenue where the dry cleaners now is. Outside the shop proudly stands Mrs. Maggie Cooper. Mr. Cooper started selling drapery from a bicycle and Cooper's first premises are seen earlier in this book. Business was transferred to this shop in 1934 and continued successfully, apart from a hiccup when the shop was bombed in the Second World War and had to be rebuilt.

28 A slightly later view of the same shop, probably late 1950s. Bill and Maggie Cooper continued to run the shop until they retired in 1960. On the right of the shop, on the corner of Orgarswick Avenue, the shop had a very popular hat stall that did very well with day trippers.

29 An excellent view of the Dymchurch Picture House built by Wheatley Bros of Goldenhurst at Aldington in 1920. This was situated opposite the City of London public house. Unfortunately the cinema was bombed in 1943 and never replaced. The nearest cinema is now at Folkestone, nine miles away. Incidentally the house known as Goldenhurst later became the home of playwright Noel Coward.

30 The City of London public house seen from the seawall. Originally called the Seawall Tavern, this pub was renamed after a ship that was blown over the seawall and into the pub during a severe storm in the 18th century. In the background on the right can just be seen the Wesleyan Chapel.

City of London. Dymchurch.

31 W.E. Coopers footwear shop next to which is Jimmy Roots express shoe repair business attached in the small building to the right. It is remarkable today to consider the range of different shops that existed in small villages and towns like Dymchurch until recent decades.

32 The main road into Dymchurch coming from Hythe. On the left is the City of London pub and opposite is the Wesleyan Chapel and in front of it Woodlands, another grocers' shop. The number of such establishments in a small town or village might seem a lot but in those days most people did their shopping locally and there were no supermarkets or out-of-town shopping developments.

THE STREET, DYMCHURCH

33 The same road looking dens and further down the road on the right are some coastguard cottages. On the left is the Lyndhurst Tea Gar-

Dymchurch, The Grove.

34 In this picture the coastguard cottages are on the left. Opposite we see an estate agents office, which also doubled as a post office and was run by Tom Neil. Adjoining the office the white weather-boarded house just visible is Wells Cottage. Further up the road the Dymchurch Garage can just be seen.

The Grove, Dymchurch.

35 A better view of Well Cottage with the post office next door. Tom Neil, the postmaster, was also a sports reporter for the Folkestone Herald from 1905, around the time this photograph was taken. Edith Nesbit sometimes stayed at Wells Cottage during her many visits to the Marsh.

Dymchurch.

Wells Cottages and Post Office.

36 Checksfields garage in about 1958. The premises seen here were built in 1952 by F. and R. Finn Bros of St. Mary's Bay. The garage business formerly operated from the opposite side of the road. The new premises incorporated a petrol filling station with a central pump island dispensing Shell, BP, Power and National Benzol. Later the site became a Shell-only station. Today the garage is still operating as a Nortons outlet. On the opposite side of the road to the garage at right angles behind the two houses is the Woodlands Dairy. To the left of the garage are the line of coastguard cottages seen in earlier photographs. These were demolished in 1963.

37 The Checksfield garage staff in 1954. Seen from left to right are Frank Cooper (secretary), Ray Barlow, Derick Woodland, David Wraight, Peter Checksfield, Ern Checksfield, Fred Morrison, George Piper, Sid Checksfield and Frank Hopkins.

38 Another view of A. Checksfield and Sons taken in about 1960. The garage appears now to be a Shell-only outlet. In the background in front of the garage is Andrew Checksfield. The cars are always interesting to see on old photographs.

39 Looking from the parish church toward the main road with the memorial in the foreground. On the opposite side of the road is a post office that was run for a short time by a Captain Austin around the early to mid-1920s. This picture is thought to have been taken around 1924. To the left can be seen another tea gardens.

THE POST OFFICE, DYMCHURCH.

40 A better view of the tea gardens and post office. Large parties were catered for here and it proved particularly popular with the large number of visitors who camped in the field behind the nearby Ship Inn. How quiet and free of traffic the main road seems.

41 The old rectory, which is now a nursing home. The kitchen Garden seems to be flourishing and the ivy on the building itself is rampant! It is surprising how many old pictures show extensive ivy growth on buildings, as if people were not so aware of the damage it was doing, or else thought the aesthetic value more important.

42 A hunt in Dymchurch, when such affairs did not attract the controversy they do today. This picture was taken on the Hythe Road and I am told may be of the East Kent Hunt from Elham, which used to meet at the Ship Inn. The hunt last met here in 1980.

43 A view of eastern Dymchurch around 1930. The field where all the cars and tents are is the Ship Field, now occupied by modern housing developments. The track across it links the Ship Inn, nearby hall and main road with the seafront. To the right of the field near the seawall can just be seen the Ship Inn vegetable gardens and slightly inland from here some private tennis courts.

44 Camping in the Ship Field in the late 1920s or 1930s. In the distance to the left can be seen the Bowery Hall, constructed in 1926 and named after a local landlord, Captain W.C. Bower. Slightly to the right beyond the conical tent is the Ship Inn, famous as the local of Russell Thorndike who wrote, and set some of his Dr. Syn stories in the pub. The Bowery Hall was, and is, used for many village functions. One notable well-known visitor was Honor Blackman, who was guest of honour at an Angling club do at the hall in 1965. Miss Blackman is best remembered for her roles as Cathy Gale, in The Avengers and Pussy Galore in the James Bond film Goldfinger.

Camping Ground, Dymchurch

210762 J.V.

45   Here the Ship Field and Wraights Field are full of campers. The Ship Inn is on the extreme left. Of particular interest in this picture is the Gypsy Caravan to be seen next to the hut at the front of the tents and caravans. Apparently this was hired out as caravan accommodation. This busy scene was captured sometime in the 1930s.

46 Another similar view of Wraights Field thought to be from the late 1930s. Although similar to the previous picture the detail makes it worth including. Among the assortment of tents, caravans and cars can be seen the Gypsy caravan to the right of the picture. Apparently up to 1000 cars could park on Wraights Field. They were usually charged one shilling per day. In 1987 Wraights Field was built upon, as new homes were constructed for the Wraight, Ritson, Welsh and Dewey families. Since then more construction has taken place to the east of this, one of the new roads being named after the French town of Salbris, with which Dymchurch was recently twinned.

47 Another nice camping scene with plenty of 1930s cars visible. The Gypsy caravan is to be seen in the background, and to the right is Barn House, the home of orchestral conductor Sterndale Bennett. This view has been approximately dated to 1934/35.

Car Park and Camping Ground, Dymchurch.

48 An early 20th century view of Meadow Cottage. The building to the right of this attractive house was a workshop containing a joiners, who made ladders and coffins among other things. On the ground floor the Wraight family had a blacksmith's business. Beyond this can be seen the haystack of Wraights farm. To the left of the workshop complex the adjoining hut was a paintshop. Standing in front of Meadow Cottage in the field is Edwin Wraight, whose grandson Bob Geering vividly remembers this scene. I am pleased to say that Meadow Cottage still stands unchanged today amidst more modern housing developments.

49 An aerial view of east Dymchurch. The Ship Inn can be seen next to its extensive field. Next to the inn can be seen tennis courts. In the middle of the field a cricket pitch can be seen. Football matches were also played in the same field. This picture also affords a good view of Sycamore Gardens. These attractive buildings were constructed between 1903 and 1912.

50 A 1920s/1930s view of the little Smugglers Tea House, which was situated to the right of the entrance to The Oval. In the 1920s a new house was built on the site.

THE SMUGGLERS' TEA HOUSE, DYMCHURCH, KENT.

51 White Gables guest house that was situated on the opposite side of The Oval entrance to the Smugglers Tea House.

White Gables also provided tea rooms open to non-residents, but was principally a hotel. The business was very successful for many years and with its distinctive appearance and thatched roof made an attractive sight on the Hythe Road. Unfortunately White Gables suffered a serious fire in the early 1970s and was never rebuilt.

52 Martello Tower number 22 opposite the white 1930s building known locally as the Wedding Cake house. The tower was demolished using high explosives in 1956 to allow for road widening. However, this proved no easy task, as initially the tower just split in two. The next attempt resulted in the debris falling across the road and blocking it for a fortnight.

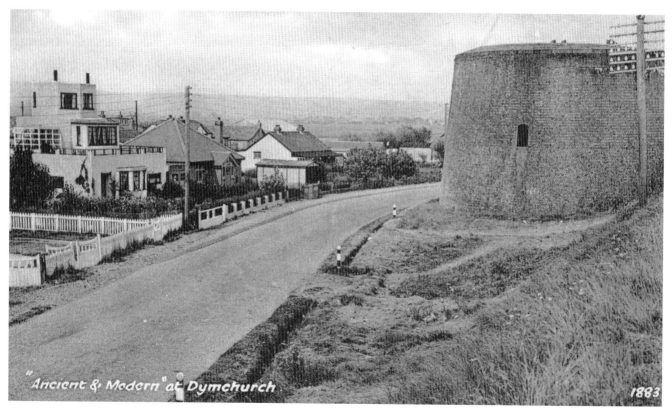

"Ancient & Modern" at Dymchurch

1883

53 The Neptune Hotel, a building of at least 16th century vintage. This attractive timber-framed house was probably a farm to start with, but has since been a coaching inn, two cottages, a public house, a tea rooms and a guest house. At present The Neptune is a nicely renovated public house with restaurant and accommodation. There are stories of smuggling associated with The Neptune. Apparently it was a popular meeting place and site for the storage of contraband destined for onward distribution.

54 The Neptune during its earlier incarnation as the MacErin Guest House. In 1999-2000 the building underwent extensive renovation and is now a popular local entertainment venue. It is said that in the 14th century a farm existed on the site prior to the present building. This apparently housed monks, who were stationed here by the Archbishop of Canterbury to work on draining and reclaiming large areas of Romney Marsh that were still partially underwater in those days.

MacErin Guest House. Dymchurch.

55 The victorious Dymchurch Football Team after winning the Hythe Charity Cup in 1958.
David Wraight, the captain, holds the cup aloft after a notable 2-1 victory over Elham Valley in the final played at Reachfields, Hythe. After being a goal down at the interval Dymchurch stormed back to notch two goals in quick succession. First, David Wraight inspired the team with a goal. Then, the fearless Peter Checksfield at left half scored with a powerful header that proved to be the winner. The team left to right are, back row: John Piper, Ian Jones and Ray Barlow.

Middle row: John Wraight, Jim Piper, Frank Williams, Geoff Eastwood, David Wraight (captain holding cup), Peter Checksfield, Roy Gearing and Cecil Wood.

In the front row is Jumbo Wraight (the Mascot).

56 The Dymchurch Football Club in 1948-1949. In the back row, left to right, are: Brian Corns, Roy Harman, Bob Gearing, Fred White, George Upton, Denis Beale and Frank Flisher. In the front row, left to right, we see: the captain David Wraight, Roy Frith, Ron Pegram and John Coates. The Dymchurch Football Club was formed in 1905 and achieved the following honours: the Hythe Charity Cup in 1948, 1958 and 1973, Folkestone and District League Division 2 in 1956/57 season, the Kent Amateur League Division 2 in 1966/67 and 1972/73, Kent Amateur League Division 1 in 1973/74, the Ashford and District League Division 2 in 1973/74, the Ashford and District League Division 2 Cup in 1974, the Kent Amateur League Division 2 Cup in 1982 and last but not least the Kent County Football League Premier League Cup in 1988. Sadly in September 1992 the club folded due to financial problems caused by the economic recession then being experienced.

57 This is The Ship Dymchurch Sunday Football Team formed in 1972. Led by manager Dave Henley the team won its first trophy in 1974, defeating the Blackhorse Sellindge 5-2 in the final of the League Cup. Goals scored were two by John Young, two by Jumbo Wraight and one by Mick Fuggle. In the 1974/75 season the team were crowned top pub side when they won the League Championship and were winners of the seven-a-side tournament held at St. Mary's Bay. The team pictured is from the 1972/73 season and consist of; back row left to right: Cliff Beverley (landlord), Jack Downey, Jumbo Wraight, Dave Tyrell, Derek Wratten, John Tolhurst, Richard Smith and Richard Williams. In the front row, left to right are: Roy Maffingham, John Young, Dave Henley (Captain), Ronnie Downey and Richard Phelps.

58 The small village of Burmarsh tucked away at the eastern end of Romney Marsh lies apart from the rush and bustle of modern times. The village clusters around its ancient church, which is flanked on the left by the old rectory and on the right by the white-washed village inn significantly named The Shepherd and Crook. This view looks east along Church Road and was probably taken in the 1920s. The Rectory can be seen on the immediate left of the picture. The road had been metalled in about 1918 prior to which it was made passable by the use of compacted beach and shingle laid by road gangs employed by the local authorities. In the late 1940s houses were built by the Romney Marsh Rural District Council on the land on the right of the photograph opposite the church.

59   A fine view of Bur-marsh Rectory standing in splendid isolation. This photograph was taken in 1887.

60 Seen from the front entrance here is Burmarsh Rectory again, this time in the 1920s. The two ladies at the front of the Rectory are believed to be the Misses Lindsay, who lived there for a number of years.

61 The church which is of Norman origin and dedicated to All Saints, consists of chancel, nave, west tower and a south porch. The churchyard is reached by crossing a dyke over a gated plank bridge, and the church is entered by way of a sunny south porch of stone, built in the 16th century. It is built on the highest ground in the village and is still regularly used for services, which are taken by the vicar from the nearby village of Dymchurch. This picture was probably taken around the turn of the century and shows in the background the village shop (part of Sankey Farm). Several burials in the churchyard resulted from a smallpox epidemic in 1779. Records show that a local carpenter, J. Wraight, was paid £5 1s 7d for the supply of coffins.

62 A winter scene of Burmarsh church taken from the rectory showing the tower with its supporting buttresses and the Shepherd and Crook in the background.

63 A view of the church with the rectory in the background probably taken before 1918, when the local roads were first metalled. The church hall, which was built in 1908, stands on land on the immediate left of the picture. Two locals can be seen sitting on the low wall which separates the churchyard from the Shepherd and Crook public house. As you can see the locals never had to walk far for a drink once the services were over!

THE CHURCH   BURMARSH.

64 A meet of the John Jones Romney Marsh Hare Coursing Club at Burmarsh outside the Shepherd and Crook. Note the bus behind them. The club was formed in 1904 and flourished for many years meeting all over the Marsh. Today, rightly or wrongly, this sport is somewhat controversial.

65 Sankey Farm taken from the footpath in the churchyard looking into Shearway (formerly Shireway). The picture was probably taken in the early 1920s. On the end of the Sankey Farm building can be seen the village shop and post office, which for many years was run by Mr. George Rayner. The main farmhouse, which dates from around 1760, was the home of Mr. Thomas Elgar and then subsequently of the Sankey family, who were local farmers and landowners, the most well known being Samuel Sankey. In recent years the building was converted into two private dwellings.

BURMARSH, DYMCHURCH

66 The village hall at Bur-marsh taken from land where there is now a housing estate known as The Green.

67   A photograph of the hub of Burmarsh village showing the church with the Shepherd and Crook pub on the right and the beginnings of Burmarsh village on the left. This picture was probably taken about 1948.

68 The severe winter of 1939-1940 in Burmarsh. These men appear to be trying to clear a path through the snow. This bad weather, the first of the Second World War, was of course a state secret as weather reports and weather forecasts, if made public, were considered to be of potential help to Hitler's Germany in planning air raids and the intended but never executed invasion of Britain.

69 How bleak and remote life must have seemed here during this severe winter weather shortly after the outbreak of the Second World War. Note how few houses there are compared to today.

70 Another bleak war-time winter scene. A few pedestrians seem to have made their way across the snow in this, perhaps the most psychologically bleak winter Britain experienced in the 20th century.

71 The sheep don't seem worried by the snow. Bur-marsh village can be seen on the horizon. Notice how much smaller Bur-marsh is compared to today when modern hous-ing developments have considerably increased its size.

72 A winters scene at Great Lathe Farm looking east showing the original farmhouse which was demolished in 1966. The cottages on the right of the photograph were Paines Cottages, which were demolished just after the Second World War. The field in the front of the photograph is now used as the car parking area for Lathe Barn Tearooms, currently under the proprietorship of Denis and Diana Wimble.

73 A small barn at Great Lathe Farm, Burmarsh. There are some very rural looking haystacks and farm implements to the left. In front of the barn is Mr. Percy Checksfield.

74 A late 1920s picture of Eaton Farm when it was owned by the Checksfield family. The present owners are Richard and Janet Andrew.

75 The Romney Hythe and Dymchurch Railway had a halt at Burmarsh Road. This was in use until October 1947 when the station closed. Since 1977, however, the platforms have again been used by schoolchildren going to Southlands Comprehensive School at New Romney. The train picks up more children at Dymchurch and St. Mary's Bay. This picture shows a 4-8-2 locomotive passing Burmarsh Halt. The photograph was taken in 1927.

BURMARSH HALT - ROMNEY, HYTHE AND DYMCHURCH RAILWAY.   No.9.

76 The Bell Ringers of Burmarsh in 1960. From left to right they are: Annie Rainer, Minnie Watts, Frank Watts, Reverend John Edinger, Mrs. Wratten, Brian Watts and Tom Fagg.